Happiness in 10 Minutes

Happiness in 10 Minutes

Brian Mountford

Winchester, U.K.
New York, U.S.A.

First published by O Books, 2006
O Books is an imprint of John Hunt Publishing Ltd.,
The Bothy, Deershot Lodge, Park Lane, Ropley, Hants, SO24 0BE, UK
office1@o-books.net
www.o-books.net

Distribution in:

UK and Europe
Orca Book Services
orders@orcabookservices.co.uk
Tel: 01202 665432
Fax: 01202 666219
Int. code (44)

USA and Canada
NBN
custserv@nbnbooks.com
Tel: 1 800 462 6420
Fax: 1 800 338 4550

Australia
Brumby Books
sales@brumbybooks.com
Tel: 61 3 9761 5535
Fax: 61 3 9761 7095

Singapore
STP
davidbuckland@tlp.com.sg
Tel: 65 6276
Fax: 65 6276 7119

South Africa
Alternative Books
altbook@peterhyde.co.za
Tel: 27 011 792 7730
Fax: 27 011 792 7787

Design: Jim Weaver Design

ISBN-13: 978 1 905047 77 2
ISBN-10: 1 905047 77 0

A CIP catalogue record for this book is available from the British Library.

Printed in the US by Maple Vail

'She often climbed up the hill and lay there alone
for the mere pleasure of feeling the wind and
of rubbing her cheeks in the grass. Generally at
such times she did not think of anything, but
lay immersed in an inarticulate well being'.

Summer, Edith Wharton

Five pillars of happiness

Realism about what's possible
Appreciation (of others and environment)
Relationship
Virtue
Purpose and meaning to life

Acknowledgements

The publisher acknowledges the following photographic sources:

Author pages 8, 62.

Fr Michael Lapsley, the Institute of Healing Memories, page 76, by kind permission.

istockphoto.com pages 14, 21, 27, 29, 35, 39, 42, 47, 54, 68, 71, 75, 82, 86, 89, 94.

Contents

Part 1

What is Happiness?

I

First thoughts

Everyone wants to be happy. The problem is we are often not clear what happiness means. Is it having health, wealth and good looks? You would think so to judge by the popular media. The icons of happiness paraded before us every day are the successful and good looking stars of TV, cinema, sport, and big business, because they are thought to be best placed to enjoy the physical pleasures that are supposed to constitute happiness. We are encouraged to inhabit the stories of their fame and vicariously enjoy their good fortune But this is misleading. Ironically, what fascinates both editor and reader alike is just as much their failure (sexual infidelities, drug habits, delinquent children) as their success. This paradox is endlessly intriguing and helps us see that happiness is more likely to be found in ordinary, everyday experience than in any fantasy.

That is not to say we shouldn't dream. To dream can be to visualise a better future and to find ways making happen, as with Martin Luther King and the civil rights movement. But in the search for happiness to dream can also mean being unrealistic or escapist, getting a high from drugs, or trying to escape dissatisfaction through alcohol, nicotine, or antidepressants. We all know that the drugs route, unless professionally managed by a medical doctor, rather than alleviating unhappiness usually incarcerates the taker in an even darker prison, the prison of addiction.

Happiness has nothing to do with being rich or handsome. We all know happy people who are neither. There has to be a different way, a deeper quality of life, which, once identified, we ought to be able to use in our search for fulfilment. This more positive approach to life is what we explore in the course of this book. We ask questions like: can we *make* ourselves happy? Can we be happy when times are hard? I think we can.

But part of the process will involve being realistic about our situation and our choices. This is hard because happiness can be volatile: one minute we're up, the next down. As we look back over our lives we can certainly identify times when we were much happier than others. There is a social pressure to be happy which encourages us to disguise our feelings. When we're asked how we are, we feel obliged if we possibly can to say, 'I'm good. I'm fine' when sometimes it would be helpful to say, 'I'm struggling'.

Happiness is always likely to be a compromise somewhere between inadequacy and perfection. The success of several TV programmes, such as the long running sitcom *Friends*, depend on this formula: the characters repeatedly make a mess of their relationships, personally and at work, in an amusing way that the viewer can identify with and find therapeutic. We don't want to be confronted by perfectly happy and emotionally successful people, but by people who at least occasionally mess up, because we recognise ourselves in their characters and their predicaments help us develop strategies for dealing with our own.

So how can we cope better? What are we aiming for and is it achievable? Not totally. Experience proves you can't know heat without cold, or light without darkness. You can't know happiness without experiencing unhappiness or other emotions of sadness, disappointment, and loss. Profound happiness and sadness are, in this case, two sides of the same coin. Our capacity to experience joy is intimately connected to the way in which we experience sorrow. This is true of all emotions; we contrast our experiences, we learn one emotion by comparison with another. A steady state of happiness would be perfect bliss, but perfect bliss would get tedious after a while. If your team always wins and never loses, football itself loses its purpose and excitement. If your favourite dinner is served to you every night with your favourite wine, your palate will become jaded, and bread and cheese will begin to seem the delicious option that could bring you happiness. As the poet Shelley wrote:

> Our sincerest laughter with some pain is fraught
> Our sweetest songs are those that tell of saddest thought.

This picture, by the young British artist Kate Bicat, addresses issues of commodity desire. Life is reflected in a shop window: the girl in the centre looks in at the fashion designs of her desire and sees herself there in intimate detail as if she were looking in the bathroom mirror. Even those who pass by are drawn into the reflection. We are looking at it but we do not see our own reflection in the glass. Or do we? What do we see represented there about happiness?

2

Happiness science

Is happiness entirely subjective, or is there a way of analysing it? To a degree we can begin to explain it scientifically through biochemistry, sociology and psychology, although the outcomes are by no means unequivocal.

1. There's a good case to be made through biochemistry that we are genetically programmed to be happy. The theory runs that since our survival depends on eating and sex, we find these things enjoyable and they make us happy. But the kind of satisfaction we get from them is designed not to last so that, however wonderful the banquet or exciting the night of passion, we are driven to seek such pleasures over and over again because they are vital to our continuing existence. The same chemical drive applies, at a more subtle level, to our

desire for financial, political, or artistic achievement, with all their concomitant advantages for us and our society: we love to be admired by our fellow human beings; success brings praise and praise makes us happy. If we found eating nauseous, sex repulsive, or praise irritating then we would be disinclined to do the very things that our survival depends upon.

Does this make you happy?

2. Sociology raises the stakes further. It looks at our physical condition – the effect of wealth and poverty, sickness and health – and finds evidence that happiness is not determined by these beyond a factor of about 10 per cent. More eating, more sex, more praise, is not in itself enough. For example, if you are starving, to be given enough money to have a good meal will greatly

increase your happiness, but once you have the bare necessities, more possessions do not make you very much happier and sometimes are the cause of worry and discontent. Surprisingly, sickness and disablement, at least after the initial crisis, does not make you significantly less happy. There is an immense resilience and optimism in the human spirit, which is probably genetic. Possibly we have a sort of median happiness point to which our brains return as a natural default.

3. Next come the psychologists, who consider whether it is possible to raise this median happiness point, or whether there is a fixed level of happiness that is part of our personality. Research[1] shows that childhood experience, especially the freedom to play creatively and having a secure relationship with parents, has immense significance in shaping the happiness of the future adult. But once grown up, can the adult do anything to improve his or her happiness? The positive-psychology movement says, yes, she can, by using such strategies as keeping a diary of positive experiences to be grateful for, or by undertaking particular acts of kindness to others. This will boost feelings of self-worth and purpose. And, they say, the greatest boost to happiness is being with other people. Belonging to a community, as people of religious faith do, and having friends, is

---

1 Paul Martin in *Making Happy People* Fourth Estate 2005

immensely important and may be the essential key to happiness. We shall consider these strategies later on.

To my mind, though, there is something unsatisfactory about such research: you expect it to explain happiness, but it doesn't, probably because it measures a 'happiness' that is necessarily superficial. You are left thinking that there must be more to it than that. Much of the material strikes me as part of what might be called a 'feel-good' approach, which idealises the 'happy' person rather as one might idealise the good-looking person. Happiness is, as it were, to have mental good looks, in the sense that it suggests there are socio-psychological fixes that can increase your happiness, in the same way that plastic surgery or Botox can (possibly) improve your looks.

3

Happiness identification test

So if eating, sex, and wealth aren't the answer, and biochemistry, sociology and psychology, while shedding light on the problem, don't solve it either, what's the key? Perhaps you can work it out for yourself. Sit down and ask yourself the question, 'what sort of life do I wish for my children?' Or, if you don't have children, 'what sort of life do I wish for the one I love?' Here is my wish list for my daughter.

- Peace of mind
- A good education
- To live a moral life in a just and fair society
- A good marriage or relationship

- Health
- An income providing enough to live on
- A sense of personal fulfilment, whatever job she pursues and whatever income she achieves
- A sense of purpose and meaning

This list, which stems from the instinctive and protective love of a parent, gives a very different spin to happiness. For all I know, it may not be what my children would wish for themselves – too staid, too middle-aged, too prescriptive, perhaps – but it points in the direction of what philosophy calls the *good life*.

4

What the philosophers say

☺

The *good life* is a phrase used by philosophers to describe what Socrates, Plato and Aristotle had to say about happiness. These three fourth-century BC Greek thinkers were closely linked; not least because Socrates taught Plato and Plato taught Aristotle. For them the good life meant leading a moral, virtuous and admirable life. Happiness was the product of virtue rather than worldly success, so that Plato was famously able to declare: the virtuous man is the happy man.

Plato particularly admired Socrates for having such total commitment to philosophy that he was willing to die for his beliefs rather than compromise them. After being found guilty on a false charge of corrupting the youth,

Socrates was sentenced to death and chose voluntarily to drink a cup of poisonous hemlock.

Aristotle took up the Platonic theme that happiness and virtue go hand in hand. He argued that happiness is related to a person's ability to fulfil their potential, and about their quality of life as a whole, not just moments of euphoria. He called it *eudaimonia*, or well-being, which means literally having a good guardian spirit or daemon. The daemon is also your true self and you are most likely to find *eudaimonia* when you strive to fulfil your potential.

Importantly, Aristotle also believed that humans have a purpose, or, as he put it, a *telos*, an end, or goal. Not from God or from a higher moral being, this purpose is embedded in nature, and it is to live a life that will inevitably involve love, friendship, reason, social relationship, and recreation. The Cambridge philosopher Simon Blackburn, whose book, *Ethics*[2], provides a brilliant summary of these ideas, jokes that 'books, concerts and bicycles are the components of many

2 Oxford University Press 2001

a good life'. He is, no doubt, thinking of his life in Cambridge (in the flat land of eastern England, where nearly everyone rides a bicycle) and in that phrase he has captured the idea of thinking, reflection, art, recreation and healthy exercise as components of the good life and therefore of happiness. If happiness and fulfilment are the products of virtuous living then we need to know what virtuous living is, what's right and what's wrong. Religion answers this problem by proposing an external moral authority, God, who reveals how we ought to behave, particularly through sacred writings such as the Bible and the Koran. Aristotle argues that, because the human purpose is embedded in nature, morality and happiness will enter our experience when nature's potential is fulfilled in us – at a crude level, when everything is working properly. There are obvious objections to this, that the destruction of the earthquake, the law of the jungle, and the virulence of disease are all natural phenomena that can cause misery.

Much later, in the eighteenth century, Immanuel Kant developed the argument, saying that we discern what is right by means of reason; that is to say, through rational consideration of what is socially necessary for humans to flourish.

Then, in the nineteenth century, Jeremy Bentham and John Stuart Mill, known as the 'Utilitarians', believed morality hung on the principle of the 'greatest happiness for the greatest number'. In an imperfect world, whatever maximises happiness for people must be good, especially where pleasure can be increased and pain reduced.

How satisfactory are these solutions? In practice, people tend to form moral opinions by a combination of some or all of these criteria: external, internal, rational and pragmatic means. I'm not going to give equal space to all these options. I want to focus on religion and particularly Christianity as a means to happiness. Obviously it doesn't always work. But it can.

5
What Christianity says

☺

1. Ought Christianity to Bring Happiness?

First it might be relevant to ask whether happiness is a proper expectation to have of religion, or whether it's just a selfish, consumerist approach to God. Besides, there's a great deal in the Christian tradition to suggest that the Christian life is about self-mortification and the suppression of the flesh; more a matter of poverty, chastity and obedience than money, sex and power. This tradition is founded in the New Testament where Jesus teaches self-denial as a means of countering the selfishness and greed that, while being part of the God-given survival instinct, can so cloud moral judgement. From time to time in Christian history self-denial has been taken to absurd extremes: the hair shirt, the assault on art at the Reformation and beyond, and the taking of male names by nuns (Sister Thomas, Sister Anselm) in order to suppress their sexuality.

The glorious Lady Chapel of Ely Cathedral originally boasted richly carved and painted walls, magnificent medieval glass, and statues adorning every niche. All these were destroyed or damaged at the English Reformation in 1539. Later, Cromwell's men smashed medieval works of art in churches, and under his Protectorate dancing, stage plays, drinking and partying were all opposed in the name of religion. In the US the Puritanism depicted in Arthur Miller's play *The Crucible* led a witch hunt not only against women, but against joy itself. This Puritanism was defined by the famous US newspaper editor HL Mencken, as 'the haunting fear that someone, somewhere may be happy'.

Such killjoy attitudes, however, seem abnormal: why should any one of us feel guilty about wanting to be happy? Doesn't the Christian tradition offer the promise of eternal happiness in heaven? What about all those 'spirituals' sung by black slaves in America, many of whom were suffering appalling abuse and exploitation? They longed for happiness: 'When I get to heaven, I'm going to dance all over God's heaven'. And surely it would be God's wish to desire the happiness of his creatures and the fulfilment of their God-given potential. He must therefore desire our happiness in the present as well as in the future.

2. Beatitude

Christianity has its own word for happiness, the somewhat archaic 'beatitude', meaning 'blessedness', which Jesus outlined in his Sermon on the Mount in Matthew's Gospel:

> 'Blessed are the poor in spirit, for theirs is the kingdom of heaven. Blessed are those who mourn, for they will be comforted. Blessed are the meek, for they will inherit the earth. Blessed are those who hunger and thirst for righteousness, for they will be filled. Blessed are the merciful, for they will receive mercy. Blessed are the pure in heart, for they will see God. Blessed are the peacemakers, for they will be called children of God. Blessed are those who are persecuted for righteousness' sake, for theirs is the kingdom of heaven.' [3]

Immediately we see that, for Jesus, happiness springs from paradoxical and upside down values, and that, as for Plato, it cannot be separated from virtuous living. Poverty, meekness and persecution hardly seems the key to happiness, yet according to this passage the combination

---

3 Matthew 5.3 onwards

of simple living, moral goodness, and endurance for the sake of principle is essential.

So what does Christianity add to the good life equation? It adds God. Loving and good by nature, God is the energy of Christian morality, infiltrating Christian action wherever the human will allows, not only setting a standard but also motivating a response. Why be good? Not in the hope of eternal reward but because it is a natural response to God's goodness. If you are able to understand God's moral influence within this kind of framework, then it will also be easy to see how God provides a moral purpose to life.

Usually expressed as, 'blessed are the poor in spirit', the first beatitude can also be translated, 'how blessed are those who know their need of God'. This subtle change of emphasis makes better sense of the puzzling 'poor in spirit', interpreting it as a state of reverence and avoiding the possible thought that it might mean 'spiritually feeble'.

Also a sense of awe in the presence of God helps a person see themselves in a broad context and not as the centre of the universe, which is one of the greatest secrets of happiness, because it forces you to get both yourself and your problems into perspective. You might even say, the bigger the God the better the perspective, because there's always a danger of reducing God to a manageable size, of making him in your own image, rather the other way round.

I would identify four aspects of awe:

1. First there is *awe at creation*. The very fact of our existence, and our consciousness, on this planet in a vast universe is totally astounding.

2. Next there is *awe at God's humility*, at the idea that God's power is expressed through the simplicity and modesty of Christ's life, 'laid in a manger, because there was no room for them in the inn'.
3. Then there is *awe at human failure*. Why when creation offers us so much do we make such a mess of it? It's important for happiness to be able to achieve self-knowledge and to own our failures.
4. And finally there is *awe at the potential of life*, whether it's awe at the miracle of new birth, being amazed at the minute perfection of a baby, or awe at God's promise of forgiveness and redemption and his challenge to us to take the risk of trying again.

Each of these experiences of awe will prompt the kind of questions that need to be faced in the pursuit of happiness, and which will be looked at more closely in the second part of this book.

6

Practical outcomes

At the level of happiness we've been talking about so far psychology, philosophy and religion have a lot in common. You could sum up their recommendations in the following list:

Count Your Blessings

Positive psychology suggests writing down a daily list of things you have felt grateful for. This helps you to look on the positive side and to see what makes your cup half full rather than half empty. Negative feelings are not nearly so depressing when counterbalanced in this way.

Positive thinking is also structured into Christianity, where giving thanks to God is the basis of prayer and worship. It is no accident that one of the best-known hymn books (and best known religious TV programmes in the UK) is entitled *Songs of Praise*.

Appreciate the Now

Closely linked with counting blessings, but with the added emphasis of being content with what we've got without covetously wishing we had more, looking over our shoulder at what we once had or worrying about what we will get in the future. Jesus gives very practical advice on this: 'do not worry about your life, what you will eat or what you will drink, or about your body, what you will wear. Is not life more than food, and the body more than clothing?' (We will look at this further in 'Enough is Enough'.)

Love your Neighbour as Yourself

This is the philosophers' *golden rule* of ethics and the key to virtuous living. Research in positive psychology shows that doing good to others actually brings happiness and therefore recommends the therapy of going out of your way to perform an act of kindness at least three times a week.

Christianity says the same in two key teachings: 'Love your neighbour as yourself', and, 'inasmuch as you do it to the least of these my brothers and sisters you do it to me'. The second of these means that our actions towards others, whether good or bad, are also actions towards God and felt by God.

Love People Not Things

The biggest danger in the pursuit of happiness is striving after the wrong thing. Psychology has shown that strong personal relationships are by far the most important happiness factor, much more important than wealth or status. If we strive for wealth and status, we are likely to be frustrated; but if we strive for good relationships and contentment, then there's a high chance of achieving the happiness we yearn for.

This is the insight of religion too: a spiritual approach to life means greater concern with spiritual rather than material prosperity. Also, relationship is a key concept in trying to understand the nature of God. Not only is God defined as Love, but God is essentially personal, thought of as a father or parent and revealed through a personal life, the life of Jesus of Nazareth, who instructed his followers to 'love one another as I have loved you'. Relationship is the oxygen of spirituality.

Show Your Gratitude

This could seem little more than an injunction to be fastidious about writing your 'thank you' letters, but it's about not taking things for granted and looking beyond our own needs to recognise the generosity of others. Positive psychology recommends the discipline of going out of our way to thank others, particularly for help at difficult times, because communicating gratitude is genuinely therapeutic.

Christianity has always emphasised the liberating effect of being open to others even when you are absorbed with your own problems.

Forgive

Don't harbour resentment, because resentment can damage your health. Unresolved conflict leads to a great deal of harmful anxiety and, given that the principle source of happiness is good relationship, the restoration of relationship through forgiveness is bound to be healing for both parties. In Christianity forgiveness is a key theme, as we shall see in 'Forgiveness and reconciliation'. Jesus was once asked by his followers how many times they should forgive each other. Would seven times be enough? He replied, no, *seventy* times seven.

Take Care of Your Body

This is the bicycle component of 'books, concerts and bicycles'. Keeping fit and trim helps us feel good and contributes to our well-being, as does a good regime of sleep and diet. While this may seem merely to state the blindingly obvious, the ill-effects of junk food, excess alcohol, and hours slumped in front of the TV show that the case isn't quite as self-evident as it might appear. There is an irony in the fact that the consumer society spawns both expensive health clubs and health and beauty newspaper supplements on the one hand, and junk-food obesity and binge drinking on the other. Health is a great boost to happiness, whereas abuse of the body is usually a symptom of a more deep-seated discontent that needs facing up to and dealing with. But health can become an obsession; beware lest a passion for muscle-tone leads to the doomed quest for eternal youth and beauty.

Judging by its track record of being hung up about sex, it might seem that the *body* is alien to Christianity, best uncelebrated and kept hidden. But, if that were true, why would God choose to become *embodied* in Jesus and experience the same bodily functions as we do: feeling, sweating, going to the lavatory. Paul, who it has to be said was probably not completely comfortable with his own

body, coined a good phrase when he described it as 'the temple of the holy spirit'. Take care of your body, because the Spirit of God can work through it, and godly values can be realised in it.

Find Strategies for Coping with Stress and Hardship

Because these things are bound to happen. Perhaps the positive psychologists should have put this first, since a bit of hard headed realism can save people from disappointment. One of the main sources of disillusion for religious people is when they discover that faith doesn't give immunity to suffering or tragedy. If you have bought in to religion on the basis that it will be an insurance policy against all things unpleasant, then you're bound at some point to be angry and disappointed. It seems that positive psychologists are saying the same thing: look for a happiness that can cope with the grim experiences of life.

Books and Concerts

Shorthand for reading, music, film, theatre and the arts in general, which are vital ingredients of recreation and morality. Through good art at least we are able explore ideas and emotions, and both the good and the evil potential of the human character. But additionally and importantly these activities, by stimulating the mind and imagination, help us to 'get out of ourselves' as we are enabled to see the world through someone else's eyes; painter, writer, or

composer. Getting out of ourselves has immense potential for making us happy as we shall see in 'Losing your life to save it'.

Part 2

Value added happiness

7

Meaning and purpose

Psychology, philosophy and religion can have a lot in common. But my purpose in this second part is to concentrate on the added dimension that religion gives, while also being open to insights from other sources such as emotional health programs.

People sometimes complain that if only they could find inspiration and purpose life would be much happier. Old age, retirement, divorce, depression, or redundancy, are just a few common conditions that can lead people to say they feel they haven't got anything to live for. Fortunately, most of the time the survival instinct drives us to look forward and to believe there will be better times ahead. But even for so-called 'successful' people there is often a fear, not far beneath the surface, that their lives don't add up to very much. You can find purpose in achievement at work, in watching your children grow up, building a house, or keeping chickens, but even if these projects are successfully accomplished, what next? We observe other living creatures, like the squirrels in our gardens, vertebrates like ourselves, industrious, struggling for survival in winter, seeming to enjoy the warmth of spring and pleasures of the mating season, but do their lives matter? Are we just a more highly sophisticated version, a by-product of evolution likely to sink without trace back into the vortex of the space and matter from which we explosively emerged?

One solution is to develop Aristotle's belief in a deep and underlying purpose, an *end* for humans on a universal scale. For Christians that transcendent purpose is God. It is well attested that finding God or a belief system is one of the pillars of human happiness, because belief in God puts you in the big picture, and gives the reassurance that you are not just a random occurrence in an evolutionary accident. God has created us in his image and desires us to fulfil that image within ourselves. His purpose is that our lives should be in complete harmony with him and since God is eternal, or outside the boundaries of time, to be in harmony with God means to have a significance and meaning that goes beyond any one individual human life.

When I conducted the funeral of the biographer and children's writer Humphrey Carpenter, who was what you might call a *devout sceptic* (probably because he was the son of a bishop), I knew that beneath the scepticism there was a deep spiritual curiosity, a curiosity indicated by the fact that he wrote biographies of CS Lewis, and Archbishop Runcie. It seemed to me that many people like him would understand the pull of transcendence and would admire Christianity for its commitment to faith in Divine Love, particularly because that Divine Love can give meaning, moral purpose, hope and eternal context to our lives; a meaning that goes beyond our birth and our death. It's a state of mind summed up in St Augustine's words referring to God, 'My soul is restless until it finds its rest in thee'.

But religious meaning is not sufficient in itself. It is not enough to say that just because God loves me I will necessarily be happy, fulfilled and full of purpose. Belief in God might meet the problem of ultimate meaning, enabling us to see ourselves in relation to divine purpose, but response is still required. Happiness is much more an active than a passive mode, and it is available at all levels of human achievement. You don't have to have been a Mother Teresa or built the Eiffel Tower for your life to be worthwhile;

ordinary, unobserved generosity, or commitment to your family or to your job is just as purposeful and fulfilling.

Hope – A Sure Sign of Purpose

To have hope is to have a sense of purpose. I think this statement makes sense, because if you believe in the good potential of the future then you have something to aim for. And, on the whole, such optimism is a natural element of our survival instinct and our capacity to bounce back after disaster and calamity. As I write, the Iraqis are electing their first full-term government since the invasion of 2003 and their President, Jalal Talabani, has expressed his 'hope for a better future' and that 'the Iraqi people will stay united'. However much the cynic might scoff at the triumph of hope over experience, without the tenacious optimism of the human spirit we would be faced with chaos and decay.

Christianity would absolutely embrace this hope, but would see it as typical of the short-term concerns in political manifestos the world over. If this is *temporal* hope, then Christianity would also want to speak of *eternal* hope.

In the period before the birth of Jesus the Jews held a widespread expectation of the coming of a messiah. It wasn't entirely clear whether this figure would be a political leader, who would liberate the Jews from Rome and restore the ancient Davidic kingdom, or a spiritual leader. When Jesus began his ministry he identified with a messianic text from Isaiah, 'the spirit of the Lord is upon me, because he has anointed me to bring good news to the poor ... to proclaim release to the captives ...'[4] His disciples didn't know exactly how to respond: one of them, Simon, was a Zealot (i.e. zealous for political liberation) and another, Judas, betrayed Jesus probably in a vain attempt to trigger a revolutionary putsch. Only when the full force of the crucifixion struck home did they realise that Jesus' liberation was spiritual. Moreover, it was in this very transcendence of worldly ambition that God effected salvation as an eternal reality. Present and future are bound together in this theological vision, as Christianity looks forward to the fulfilment of God's temporal creation, confident in the belief that God has already begun the redemption of all people in the life, death and resurrection of Jesus. The fullness of life is yet to come. In the present we see through a glass darkly, but then, at the end time, we shall see face to face, as St Paul says in the same chapter that he identifies hope, along with faith and love, as the sovereign virtues.[5]

The hope that St Paul talked about, however, was a hope that comes from the assurance that the individual will ultimately be united with God: 'in hope we were saved. Now hope that is seen is not hope. For who hopes

---

4 Luke 4.18 Isaiah 61.1-2

5 1 Corinthians 13

for what is seen?'[6] God is the hope of the future providing the hope of a personal salvation, which is an immense support for many people. But eternal salvation, like human rights, comes with responsibilities since hope also involves judgement. Isaiah first condemns the oppression of the poor, before giving the Jews in exile hope of getting home to Jerusalem. In the wonderful poetry of Isaiah 35, he says that the wilderness and the dry land shall be glad; the desert shall rejoice and blossom like the crocus. Then he continues: God will come with vengeance, with terrible recompense. 'The eyes of the blind shall be opened, and the ears of the deaf unstopped; then the lame shall leap like a deer, and the tongue of the speechless sing for joy'. Basically, you can't have hope without judgement because hope can never be grounded in wishful thinking or lazy ethics. It must result in social action or it will be meaningless. We have to see that we live in the real world of human nastiness where the outworking of hope can only be realised by radical change. This means facing the moral scars on our own social landscape – war, the prisons, urban violence, pornography, internet grooming, our unrepentant exploitation of the environment, the compensation culture, the indifference to poverty and suffering that is not our own.

I think of hope as a combination of faith, optimism and determination: faith that God is there as a good and

---

6 Romans 8.24

benign influence; the disposition to be positive rather than negative; and a will not to be defeated. We often see the effectiveness of this hope in extreme situations: when a person copes with serious illness, or faces with courage what seems to the rest of us a disproportionate share of tragedy; or someone like Terry Waite, who found enough hope to withstand five years solitary confinement as a hostage in Beirut.

8

Great expectations

One summer's day I received a visit from two-year-old Chloe, who has an interest in vegetable gardening. Seeing ripe tomatoes in the greenhouse, she expressed her desire to pick them. So I fetched a polythene freezer bag and she picked the four finest fruits, which we placed very carefully into the bag. The idea was that she'd take them home to Mummy as a nice surprise. While she was saying goodbye, I thought she was holding the tomatoes rather too casually and I said, 'For goodness sake *don't drop the tomatoes*'. Immediately, right on cue, she dropped them splat on the floor. All the adults present turned out to be star amateur child-psychologists who, for some reason, found the misfortune of my tomatoes immensely amusing.

They were quick to observe that it is foolish to introduce a child to negative thoughts, and that one must always be positive. You say, 'Hold tight to the tomatoes', but never 'don't drop the tomatoes'. So I packed another four of the pulpy red fruits into a bag and said, 'Chloe, hold tight to the tomatoes', and her little hand grasped the polythene like a vice, as she threw me a sideways glance akin to mockery. This parable illustrates how important our expectations of each other actually are and how deep-seated our response to what others expect of us is. To take another example from the grown-up world; contrast these two approaches of an employer to an employee when allocating tasks:

1. I am not sure that I should give you this responsibility because you are not really up to it.
2. Here is a challenge that I believe you can rise to and I want you to give it your best shot.

Which is likelier to get the best from the employee and ultimately which will make employer and employee happier? What we expect from one another, and what we hope others will expect from us, is important in the process of happiness. To expect little is to *belittle* a person, whereas to expect positive response is both affirming and encouraging.

Christian reflection has made a theology out of this. It says that God created us with the potential for goodness and that God does us the honour of expecting us to fulfil this potential. The clear view of the biblical writers is that God created us in his own image, whether you read Genesis, 'let us make humankind according to our likeness', or St Paul who describes a convert as being clothed with a 'new self' made according to 'the image of its creator'[7]. Being made in God's image carries with it duties, particularly the keeping of God's commandments. Rather than feeling any sense of resentment that we are expected to live by God's standards, we should feel affirmed that God believes we are capable of such high achievement, rather like the employee being asked to rise to the challenge. This affirmation leads to the same kind of happiness we experience when receiving support and approval from parents, spouse, or boss.

---

7 Colossians 3

9

Losing your life to save it

As in all aspects of life, the path to happiness is not without its paradoxes, even for persons made in the image of God. All four gospels highlight Jesus' declaration that 'those who want to save their life will lose it, and those who lose their life for my sake ... will save it'.[8] What a curious contradiction. Surely the search for happiness means getting life rather than losing it. But the paradox works on at least two levels. First, there is the literal sense of actually sacrificing life for someone else; the rescuer who enters the burning building, or the swimmer who dives into the sea to save a drowning man, and in the process loses his or her

8 Luke 9.24

own life. We admire the nobility of such an act and heap honour on the person who makes it. As it says in the Bible, 'no one has greater love than this, to lay down one's life for one's friends'.[9] And that is a model for many other lesser sacrifices made for the sake of others, whether it's caring for an elderly relative, donating a kidney, or turning down a job opportunity because your family is too settled to move to another town.

In a second sense losing your life to save it can mean foregoing the superficial consumerist pleasures of the marketplace in order to discover the delights of something deeper. By way of illustration, I ask myself what I think makes for a happy childhood. Not having loads of luxuries, computers, TVs, and electronic games (although these things have their place). A happy childhood depends rather on the expansion of the imagination through the invention of games and make-believe: a child's bed becomes a ship offering safety in the teeth of a storm or a few kitchen chairs become a castle against the adult world. Not only does such experience help to create the wonder of childhood, it is a building block of happiness, because the imagination is an inner resource through which the selfish ego can be controlled. Through the lens of imagination the individual is led into a free and liberating world of exploration and personal development, which of course can also be true for

---

9 John 15.13

adults, as we have seen, through film, theatre, music and art, and especially through reading, where the imagination is forced to create pictures of its own and to add flesh and bones to the characterisation on the written page.

Simone Weil, the French philosopher and mystic of the early twentieth century, believed that an essential part of prayer was to forget the self in order to concentrate on God. She suggested that an example of effective self-forgetfulness is to be found in doing mathematical exercises, because the mind becomes so absorbed with solving the problem that any self-interest is temporarily lost.

This is what positive psychologist, Mihaly Csikszent-mihalyi (pronounced chick-sent-me-high-ee), calls a 'flow state', when people are so fully absorbed in an activity that they lose their sense of time and have feelings of great satisfaction. Csikszentmihalyi describes *flow* as 'being completely involved in an activity for its own sake. The ego falls away. Time flies. Every action, movement, and thought follows inevitably from the previous one, like playing jazz. Your whole being is involved, and you're using your skills to the utmost.'[10] Put simply it means getting out a bit, joining a club or society, finding a hobby, allowing yourself to be absorbed by something else. For me, it's woodwork: drawing a plan, sharpening the chisel and the blade of the plane, choosing the wood, cutting pieces to size with care and accuracy, watching the object or piece of furniture gradually take shape. The co-ordination of hand and eye requires an all absorbing concentration such that when you take a break you realise that other worries and concerns have been temporarily suspended and you may even see them, as a result, in a different light.

I have noticed, and I wonder if it is a coincidence, that craftsmen very often have a calm, good-natured and good-humoured temperament. A carpenter of my acquaintance always has a ready smile and is interested in any problem you set before him. He has a tool for everything from cutting architrave for damaged Victorian doors to restoring the

---

10 *Flow: The Psychology of Optimal Experience*, Csikszentmihalyi M – New York: Harper & Row (1993).

broken tail fin on a wooden fish; and if he doesn't have it he will make it. Flow is part of the carpenter's job description. I can't resist the observation that Jesus of Nazareth was a carpenter who learnt the trade from his father, Joseph.

Iris Murdoch, who was an Oxford philosophy don before she became a novelist, points out that Plato believed that the *technai*, the arts and crafts, can help us to see what is most excellent in reality. She says, 'the appreciation of beauty in art or nature is not only the easiest available spiritual exercise; it is also a completely adequate entry into the good life, since it is the checking of selfishness in the interest of seeing the real'.[11] Her argument is that a great artist is able to stand back and see her subject with a degree of detachment in which selfish concerns vanish and nothing exists except the object or person being contemplated. We would be able to tell the difference between good and bad art by distinguishing whether a picture depicts an honest reality or a sentimental, consolatory, sugary one.

If it's difficult to get into the mind of the artist without being an artist oneself, it is easier to understand the point in relation to music. You go to a concert, whether classical or pop, and you might have the sensation of losing yourself in the sound. Listening to music isn't easy, it requires effort and concentration – at least it demands time, which we don't have much of – to let your inner self be filled with

---

11 *The Sovereignty of Good* – Iris Murdoch – RKP 1970

music. It's like prayer, like spiritual contemplation, letting the *other* in.

What we are saying is that happiness requires a proportion of personal discipline and unselfishness. It is not available pre-packed and ready-made as some advertisers would have us believe; obtainable through a price reduction, a sunny beach abroad, or a seductive perfume. It is much more likely to be found in making the effort to be free of the pull of short-term material solutions and getting involved in activities that 'get you out of yourself'.

10

Coping with suffering

To sum up this section so far: religion provides hope, and a means of fulfilling our potential; it offers a theology of self-giving and generosity; can it also be help us to deal with the problems of pain and suffering?

The answer must depend partly on how great the pain is: it is extremely unlikely that a prisoner suffering systematic torture would claim to be happy, but on the other hand there are many people suffering from chronic arthritis, and other painful chronic disabilities, who live very happy lives. Nevertheless, in the technological culture, pain is seen as inimical to happiness. Just as we expect to eat salad all year round, whatever the cost to the environment, so we expect the doctor and the dentist to dispense analgesics to numb our pain as and when we want.

A similar attitude can also too easily be taken towards God. The existence of evil and suffering is the classic objection to the existence of God. Assuming that benevolence and omnipotence are amongst God's attributes (which not all religions do: the Hindu Shiva is both good and evil), then how can an all-loving, all-powerful God permit suffering? Either God is not benevolent, not all-powerful, or suffering does not exist. The latter suggestion seems absurd, although there are those who argue that in the context of the big picture of creation suffering is an incidental factor. They sometimes draw an analogy with dissonance in music, where beauty is created through the clash between dissonance and harmony, as it were pain and resolution. A more popular answer to the problem is that having created the world, God gave us free will, so it's all our own fault really. But if that's the case how do we explain the suffering caused by natural events like tsunamis and volcanoes, which clearly are not our fault?

We need to be able to see that suffering and happiness are not mutually exclusive, because pain, in some form or another, is a reality that will visit us all. Suffering cannot be regarded as the greatest enemy of happiness; it has to be embraced, not necessarily welcomed, but we need to learn how to give space to vulnerability. George Eliot wrote in her novel, *Ramola*,

> 'It is only a poor sort of happiness that could ever come by caring very much about our own narrow pleasures. We can only have the highest happiness ... by having wide thoughts, and much feeling for the rest of the world, as well as ourselves; and this sort of happiness often brings so much pain with it, that we can only tell it from pain by its being what we would choose before everything else, because our souls see it is good.'

An important component of happiness is the ability to take on board the reality of unhappiness, because once a problem is recognised it is much easier to deal with it, however daunting the prospect. Suffering requires realism and if it diminishes us, then we must use our best human resources, both practical and moral, to humanise it. We have a natural ability to do this – we call it resilience and courage – a fact that is evidenced by psychological research that shows that serious illness does not cause disproportionate unhappiness.

Cognitive Behaviour Therapy

One technique for coming to terms with the reality of a problem is cognitive behaviour therapy. Basically, this helps weaken the connections between troublesome situations and habitual reactions to them, such as fear, depression, or rage. It also teaches how to calm the mind and body, in order to feel better, think more clearly, and make better decisions. And it shows how certain patterns of thinking can give a distorted picture of what's going on in life, making a person anxious, depressed or angry for no good reason. Cognitive behaviour therapy can provide very powerful tools for dealing with symptoms and getting life onto a happier footing. However, for advice it is best to consult a medical doctor.

Suffering at the Heart of Christian Spirituality

The paradox of the Christian God, whom we generally think of as so powerful and effective that he was able to create the world, is that, when reflected in the life of Jesus, that same God is also vulnerable and suffers an appalling death by crucifixion. This fact puts suffering at the heart of Christian spirituality, where it reflects a very different view of happiness. The paradox had seemed ludicrous

right from the beginning: Paul wrote to the Corinthians that the idea of a crucified God was a 'stumbling block to the Jews and foolishness to the Gentiles'[12]. But he added that God's weakness is stronger than any human strength. This gives a different view of God, not so much the great problem solver or universal remedy for ills, but the one who by suffering *with us* helps us to solve our own problems. God, you might say, is in the wound not in the bandage.

As we saw in 'Losing your life to save it', a favourite gospel image is that of 'taking up your cross' to follow Christ. This suggests the embracing of suffering on the road to happiness. The Archbishop of Canterbury has defined the religious life for the individual as 'taking on the task of ensuring a place for God'. But what is the character of that God? Is it not a vulnerable divine presence? The emotionally healthy individual learns to embrace suffering, and to try to absorb it, in order to transform it into part of the wholeness of being. While we work to eradicate suffering through medicine, education and political justice, we must allow a space for the suffering that is an inevitable and natural part of our lives, not try to sweep it under the carpet, pretending it doesn't exist, because to do so would merely be to conspire with a secular society that tends to regard suffering as an abnormality or embarrassment, in

---

12 1 Corinthians 1.23

the same sort of way that it regards old age and poverty as an embarrassment.

While emphasising the importance of taking a realistic approach towards suffering, I wouldn't wish to undervalue that wonderful natural defence mechanism, selective memory, which filters out many of our painful experiences. Although we speak of happiness as if it were a condition of the present, a lot of happiness involves retrospection, looking back at good times past when all was well and we prospered and probably it was summer and the sun was shining. I wouldn't for a moment belittle this as nostalgia, or mock it as looking at the world through rose-tinted spectacles, because it's surely natural and healthy. Just imagine how valuable selective memory is for a person recovering from a traumatic experience, or for the old person who, having outlived friends and relatives, and feeling the aches and pains of age, finds happiness in sweet memory.

11

Emotional well-being and sound relationships

Now is the moment to look more closely at that fundamental key to personal happiness, relationship. Whether it's in the family, in marriage or partnership, at work, at leisure, or in the church community, how we relate to one another is fundamental to our well-being and that of others around us. Are there, therefore, strategies for making good relationships or for improving relationships that are unsatisfactory? Silly question: just Google 'relationship skills' and you'll come up with 22 million sites, many of which represent professional programmes aimed at emotional health and literacy. Here we look at four basic constructs that can help.

1. Empathy

Empathy is the ability to understand another person's feelings and to try to share their emotional experience. It involves the management of the ego and the control of that childish 'me first' instinct that can so easily blind us to needs of others. To be empathic will make others open to you, and like you, because the sense of being heard, being understood and being cared about is liberating both for adults and children alike and always nurtures the growth of relationship.

Empathy is well illustrated in relation to children because, although we have all been children, we often find it difficult to understand the child's inner world and therefore have to make a conscious effort to think in their terms and get into their mind set in order to connect. When we are able to recognise their fears and see the validity of their emotional point of view, our relationship with them will be happier and closer. This works because people who are treated with respect and empathy grow to treat others in the same way. Sadly the reverse is also true and many who behave abusively do so because they've been on the receiving end of emotional indifference or disrespect.

When the tsunami struck at the end of 2004, we saw an amazing empathic reaction as millions of people around the world identified with the suffering of the individuals and communities involved and responded with extraordinary financial generosity.

In Christian ethics empathy is important too and perhaps best summed up in St Paul's chapter about love in 1 Corinthians 13 where he says love is patient, kind, not envious or boastful, arrogant or rude. It does not insist on its own way; it bears all things, believes all things, hopes all things, and endures all things.

2. Appreciation Makes People Happy

There's an exercise popular with teamwork trainers and group therapists that involves participants having a piece of paper pinned to their back on which the others must write something appreciative about the wearer. It's a way of drawing out positive thoughts rather than negative ones and of helping people to see the good in each other rather than the bad. This focus on appreciation and affirmation we call 'positive behaviour' and it's remarkable how it brings out the best in people.

Again we can learn from the application of this technique in the education of children. When disruptive behaviour is met with anger and ridicule the conflict between adult and child tends to escalate, leading to increasingly unacceptable behaviour and lowering of self esteem on the part of the child, which can be as damaging as physical punishment. On the other hand, where positive techniques are used there can be dramatic improvements: whole schools have been turned around from classroom anarchy into happy communities by this method. The technique is to use praise and rewards for good behaviour, because what we pay attention to is what we get more of; giving responsibility to the child; and making the child aware that s/he has a choice how to behave but must be ready to face the consequences of that decision in a context where discipline is fair and consistent.

Is the adult world so different? I don't think so. Whether it's a woman coyly telling her suitor that flattery will get him nowhere (but not meaning it), or a colleague admiring a piece of work you have done, we are all built up, cheered, and contented by appreciation.

3. Self-awareness and Self-esteem

It's often said, but no less true for having been said often, that to love others we must first learn to love ourselves. Being sensitive to our own needs, and taking responsibility for them, helps us be more nurturing towards others. If we don't like who we are, or if we have unresolved hang ups about past experience, then this is very likely to impair our relationships with others, since these chronic self-concerns are going to make it almost impossible to empathise and see things from their point of view.

There is a paradox here: having argued that the suppression of the ego is relationship-enhancing, now we are saying that we must learn to love ourselves. It might help allay that apparent contradiction to say that there is a difference between egocentricity and self-respect, which has something to do with the difference between immaturity and maturity, self-absorption and proper self-esteem. The dilemma has not passed unnoticed in Christian ethics, where there has been criticism of the idea that Christian love requires negation of self. Feminist theologians, for example, have argued that the tradition of self-negation in Christianity has assisted the oppression of women in church and society, and the same could be argued for all oppressed groups. Surrender of self endangers the development of personhood and part of God's love for us is that he desires the fulfilment of our potential – to be the best that we can be.

4. Humour

Try to picture happiness and, more than likely, you'll come up with a laughing or smiling face, so it may seem perverse that I haven't until now mentioned the part that humour plays in a happy life.

When I was a child, my parents took the *Reader's Digest*, which contained a regular feature, 'Laughter is the best medicine'. For a reward of £5 for published letters, readers were invited to submit an amusing story or anecdote, because laughter 'makes you feel better'. Since that time research has shown that laughter does indeed have a beneficial chemical effect by releasing endorphins into the blood, which in turn relieve pain and reduce stress, and by producing serotonin, a substance that helps to modulate mood and improve sleep and appetite.

But there is a chicken and egg problem here: does laughter make you happy, or does being happy make you laugh? Both statements are true, I think, and we implicitly recognise laughter's ability to help us cope with the common phrase, 'Well, you've got to laugh!'

Looking at laughter from another perspective, to be able to laugh at yourself is important. How virtuous it is to recognise your own faults, and not to take yourself too seriously. I call it the laughter of hope because any individual or organisation that cannot laugh at itself, at least sometimes, is suffering from a humour haemorrhage that is likely to be emotionally and spiritually fatal.

Jesus never laughed, at least that was the opinion of

St John Chrysostom in the fourth century, presumably because to do so might appear to undermine the gravity of his message on such matters as sin and repentance. Consequently Christianity has generally been anti laughter. But the Jesus portrayed in the gospels seems to me to have had a sense of humour. Did he not laugh when he partied and ate with publicans and sinners? Did he not smile when he told the story of the wise and foolish virgins or the woman relentlessly banging on the judge's door at midnight? Did he not have a humorous dig at those who took their religion too seriously – you strain a gnat (out of your drink, to keep ritual law) but swallow a camel![13] It's the same joke as the camel and the eye of a needle – the humour of overstatement and hyperbole. It pricks the bubble of pomposity and over serious self-regard, like the story of the bishop who is guest speaker at a local church and when he arrives he finds scarcely anyone there. So he says to the minister, 'Didn't you tell them I was coming?' and the minister replies, 'No I didn't say a thing, but the word must have got out'.

---

13 Matthew 23.24

12
Sex

To state the blindingly obvious, a good sexual relationship makes you happy, because it's pleasurable and exciting, and because it's personally affirming when someone else is willing to be intimate with you. All five senses communicate its delights: touch, sight, smell (pheromones and perfumes with names like 'temptation'), taste (kissing), and hearing (the language of love and the whisperings of sweet nothings). Beyond this immediately personal and physical experience lies an even more subtle layer of enjoyment experienced through the imagination, for example, in the pleasure of reading a love story in a novel or watching the portrayal of relationship in a film.

But just as sex has all this potential for pleasure and happiness, so it can be a cruel tormentor. The cruelty of it is that nature drives us to want it even when it's hard to get – no one fancies me, society forbids it, or I'm too old. There are substitutes and consolations, particularly through the visual senses in what you might call the 'lens love' of magazines and the internet, but they usually fail to satisfy in any personal way and, while they might begin with a harmless delight in human beauty, they often lead to the distortion of pornography.

Since our survival instincts are so strong and potentially difficult to control, all societies impose limits on sexual behaviour, such as the age of consent, legal marriage, the outlawing of bigamy and incest, clothing customs like the Muslim hijab, single sex changing rooms, or initiation rites like circumcision. These rules and customs have evolved for the well-being and common good of particular societies, although that doesn't mean they are right always and everywhere and can never be questioned. The practice of female circumcision is now widely regarded as abusive and the imposition of certain dress codes thought by many to be repressive.

Strings Attached

Christian marriage itself provides a restrictive moral framework, based on the belief that sexual relationship flourishes in the context of lifelong commitment and responsibility between partners, with the primary purpose of bearing and bringing up children in a family. These ideas are enshrined in the historic wedding service, which sets out three objects for marriage: the procreation of children, the maintenance of a monogamous social order, and, less bleakly, friendship between man and wife – 'mutual society, help and comfort in prosperity and adversity'. In more modern versions this order has been changed, so that friendship comes first, the care and upbringing of children second, and the maintenance of social order third; but using gentler words: marriage 'enriches society and strengthens community'. This change of order and vocabulary goes some way to recognising the shifting mores of a contemporary, globalised society in which a monocultural approach is no longer possible. Like most ethical and theological issues, marriage cannot be reduced to a simplistic formula. The ethical response needs to be sensitive to a range of human conditions, such as the fact that many people cannot have children as a result of infertility, and what an emotional wilderness that can lead to; also that some people choose not to have children, usually for reasons other than hedonistic selfishness, a decision that deserves our trust. Indeed, on a planet with a population of 6.4 billion people, expected to double by 2050, the idea that having kids is an intrinsic good is going to have to be reviewed, and we could all end up with a Chinese style limitation on our procreativity. In a similar and parallel line of moral reasoning, we ought to be sensitive to a person's sexual orientation and glad that civil partnership is also based on mutual commitment and respect.

While lifelong commitment is the Christian ideal, we now recognise that relationships don't always work out, aren't always based on real compatibility; people change, things go wrong. And divorce and remarriage is often the answer. The Church has come slowly and reluctantly to recognise the importance of forgiveness, realism, and acceptance in the matter of marital breakdown.

But lifelong commitment remains the goal and aspiration. The Church would certainly encourage people to work at their marriage when times are difficult and not to give up lightly, recognising that it is 'for better and for worse'; not to treat it like another consumer product, a TV or a car that can be traded-in on a whim for a later model without thought to the consequences.

The real genius of Christian marriage, it seems to me, and its lasting gift to the understanding of human relations, is the insistence that happy and fulfilled relationship is most likely to result from self-giving love faithfully sustained through good times and bad. Many people, including many Christians, recognise that this formula is true not only for marriage but for *every kind of relationship*, whether sexual or platonic, inside or outside marriage, parental or filial. And, although the Church is divided on the issue, a very significant proportion of Christians recognise the validity of gay and second marriage relationships as also being harmonious with the character of love that comes from God.

It's not always easy to accept the rigours of this analysis, despite the centuries of experience behind it, and the temptation to look for happiness, fun and excitement in a variety of sexual encounters is a recurring theme in human affairs. Two people might agree that they will have a relationship with 'no strings attached'. Usually they're married or in relationship with someone else. We'll just enjoy the sex, they say, and carry on as usual. But emotional strings always attach themselves, whether through jealousy, guilt, or the desire of the supposedly free lovers to make commitments, to be together more, even have a child.

Christian Ambivalence about Sex

Despite the fact that Christianity has a cheering and honest view of marriage (in the pre-Reformation English service, a bride would promise to be 'bonny and buxom at bed and at board') the history of its attitude to sex generally has been kill-joy rather than celebratory. Jesus had little to say about it that was recorded. His most telling comment is when he is asked to give judgement on a woman about to be stoned for adultery. After some thought, he tells her accusers that whoever amongst them has no sin should cast the first stone. Thus he makes forgiveness his priority and, one would like to think, is also expressing abhorrence at the barbarism of stoning. St Paul, on the other hand, is more negative, influenced by the lax sexual morals in the city of Corinth, where he founded a church, and by his belief in the impending end of the world. What's the point of marriage, he asks, if God's Judgement is coming in a matter of months? Wouldn't it be better to concentrate on making spiritual preparation?

This teaching, the result of a particular and short-lived eschatological view, became the root of the early Western Church's belief that virginity was morally superior to marriage, and the consequent insistence on the celibacy of the clergy. Further wariness about sex is added by the pre-scientific, Aristotelian view of human biology, which held that the male sperm is the whole potential embryo and that the womb is simply the garden in which it grows (which helps to explain the virgin birth of Jesus) and therefore anything interfering with the development of the male seed, such as masturbation, contraception, or same sex relations is murder.

In the fourth century, Augustine of Hippo regarded the desires of lustful sexuality as the epitome of a disorder that

entered the world at the moment Adam and Eve knew they were naked. Church historian, Diarmaid MacCulloch writes, 'Augustine speculated wistfully about the time before the Fall in Eden, when Adam and Eve's private parts behaved in an orderly fashion. The Church has been trying to tell private parts what to do ever since'.

Conclusion

The heart of relationship is friendship and a genuine desire for the well-being of another person; the physical side of relationship is secondary. One of the problems for contemporary culture in the West is that the pervasive presentation, through advertising and media, of sex as bodily function downgrades relational integrity and puts unrealistic ideals of physical beauty before us as a norm that can easily induce feelings of inadequacy and create illusions that most people are enjoying wonderful sex and that if you are not, then you're pretty sad.

As far as the physical is concerned, all relationship is physical at some level, and what Christianity proposes is the idea that the physical is a *sacrament* of the relationship, by which it means the physical expression of a deeper inward emotion. So that a mother cradling her child in her arms is a sacrament of the commitment of mother-love; friends embracing is a sacrament of their companionship; and sexual relations is a sacrament of personal commitment and intimacy. And constancy is an important part of all this. As Shakespeare says in his 116th Sonnet: 'Love is not love, Which alters when it alteration finds'

and then the famous lines:

> 'Love's not Time's fool, though rosy lips and cheeks
> Within his bending sickle's compass come;
> Love alters not with his brief hours and weeks,
> But bears it out even to the edge of doom.
> If this be error and upon me proved,
> I never writ, nor no man ever loved.'

13

Forgiveness and reconciliation

When I was a first a minister in North London and an arrogant young fellow to boot, I had a public row with my church treasurer about some financial matter, which ended in unkind things being said. I've always hated letting the sun go down on my wrath and later that evening I was fretting so much that at 11pm I went round to his house to apologise. He too had been sitting up worrying and he immediately invited me in for a whisky. It was an event that created a bond between us that never weakened and I realised how difficult it is to be happy in a state of antagonism.

It's a rare person who has never reached deadlock in a quarrel, whether with a partner, a colleague or neighbour. The experience can be hurtful and infuriating, but if the situation is not dealt with it will fester and lead to more damaging problems. Someone has to give ground, say 'I'm sorry' and *mean* it.

But it is essential to realise that forgiveness is never easy and always costs. We've all seen the stroppy child being pressed to apologise by a parent for some misdemeanour and after hours of resistance eventually mouthing a resentful 'sor-ry', with an ironic emphasis on both syllables. You know at once that the problem hasn't really been resolved. Fr Michael Lapsley of the Institute of Healing Memories in South Africa, calls this 'bicycle theology'. You steal someone's bicycle and after six months feel guilty and say sorry, and the person you've stolen it from says that's OK, but you still keep the bicycle. You've got to be able to give the bicycle back, because reparation is important. When a relationship has been poisoned by hurtful things being said or done, the poison has to be drawn through genuine remorse and forgiveness and not feeling able to do this is bound to lead to unhappiness.

Dealing with the Past

Basically, forgiveness and reconciliation is about how we deal with the past. How are we going to deal with difficult childhood memories, past failures, or feelings of hatred and revenge, and how can we deal with the haunting memories that bring shame and regret? At one level we dwell on the past and want to sort it out because it comes back to trouble us; but at another we want to sweep it under the carpet and move on. The day Nelson Mandela walked out of prison he said nothing about revenge or retribution, despite the fact that those who imprisoned him had made him work in a quarry until his eyes were permanently damaged by rock dust, and all because he simply wanted justice. He knew that there are more important things than to complain about the past or to harbour resentment because that would be the way of extending the cruelty of his captors, extending his prison sentence, when at last he had freedom. No one could imagine that this was easy for him, but equally one can see that he was right.

Christianity adds another dimension. While it's big on forgiveness and reconciliation, it's also big on memory and memorialising. It makes a virtue out of memory, because it views history as a harmonious unity under God. So, the central feature of Christian worship is a re-enactment of the Last Supper, in which Jesus took bread and wine, said they were his body and blood, and told his disciples, in the future, to break bread in memory of him. Although this memory is of the cruel execution of an innocent man, it is also a redemptive and transforming memory in that it recalls the good that can come out of evil. Jesus forgave the soldiers who hammered the nails into his hands with the words, 'Father, forgive them for they know not what they do'. The manner in which he accepted the pain and cruelty of his death stands as an icon for the triumph of love over evil, revealing, Christians believe, both the nature of God and the potential for universal healing and forgiveness through the resurrection.

Healing Memory

The brilliance of Fr Michael Lapsley's insight is to see that destructive memory can be healed rather than merely left behind or hidden. His own story is his best illustration.

As a priest standing against apartheid in President de Clerk's South Africa, he received a parcel bomb that blew off his hands and blinded him in one eye. How was he to cope with the memory of this terrible event? He had no one to forgive because he didn't know who sent the bomb. He writes, 'I am not full of hatred, I'm not bitter, I don't want revenge. Because I realise that if I am filled with hatred and bitterness I would be a victim for ever; they would have failed to kill the body, but they would have killed the soul'. The memory of his dreadful experience, with its ever-present reminders, inspired him to found an Institute to help others heal their own memories. So *a fortiori*, if forgiveness and healing can work in extreme situations like those of Michael Lapsley and Nelson Mandela, then it can work in all lesser situations and their experience and response is a challenge to everyone else.

People and Nations

What applies to individuals also applies to groups and nations. We are very familiar with the ancient feuds and resentful memories that continue to plague whole societies today: the ongoing feud between Catholic and Protestants in Northern Ireland, the Arab/Israeli conflict in Israel/Palestine, one group claiming their 'Promised Land' the other resenting being ousted from a land they had occupied for over a thousand years, or the Hutus massacre of the Tutsis in Rwanda, revenging old grievances. We might also think of the Iraq War in which thousands of Iraqis died in the aftermath of 9/11, a terrorist outrage that they had nothing to do with, reflecting a tension between 'Christian' West and 'Muslim' East that goes back to the Crusades.

These are feuds that have brought incalculable misery to people in different parts of the world. How are they to be resolved and healed? It is much more difficult for a group or nation to give back the bicycle. We have had heads of state making public apology for the past wrongs of their people, and this goes some way towards reconciliation, but how can you be sure that everyone really means it? You can't. But this difficulty of taking corporate responsibility cannot be an excuse for just leaving things as they are, unresolved. It requires a particular form of political determination for justice, often expressed by people on the fringe of political power – the rebel, the prophetic outcast – to prick the national conscience and force change.

Four Steps Towards Healing

Christian theology is thoroughly realistic about human failings and the inadequacy of the political process, recognising that we are imperfect and constantly mess up. It teaches that the purpose of God's becoming human in the life of Jesus Christ was to restore a right relationship between God and humanity, a relationship that had been spoiled by sin. This is what is meant by the phrase that

Jesus 'takes away the sins of the world'. The restorative forgiveness that God offers is total. When a sin is cancelled it is cancelled for good and no resentment lingers in the mind of God. But, again, this is not offered as an easy solution, or as we sometimes say, 'cheap grace'. There is a required process of repentance, the basis of which would be accepted by many a religious and humanist person alike.

1. Telling the truth. The first essential is to be honest about the wrong I have committed and to acknowledge the hurt I have caused. Without that basic realism there can be little hope of revitalising relationship.
2. Repentance. Secondly, having acknowledged my action I need to show a genuine change of heart and determination not to do it again.
3. Restitution. Wherever possible I need to restore what has been damaged or destroyed, to give the bicycle back. But it's more subtle than just returning stolen goods: I need to see how I can restore the dignity of the person I have humiliated, or the love of the partner I've wronged, or repair the environment I have plundered.
4. Reconciliation. Maybe in practice the three previous points merge into one because they each represent a part of the process of reconciliation. We might reasonably hope that the person with whom I hope to be reconciled will not wait until I've achieved truth,

> repentance and restitution, but will come at least some way to meet me. Reconciliation is a two-way thing and to make the effort of repentance usually melts the heart of the other person. In Jesus' parable of the Prodigal Son repentance melts the heart of God[14]. The wastrel son repents of squandering his father's money in a far country and resolves to ask forgiveness. 'I will go to my father and say I have sinned against heaven and before you and am no longer worthy to be called your son'. As the boy approaches home his father goes out to meet him and embraces him and puts a ring on his finger and kills the fatted calf to celebrate his return.

Given that good relationship is one of the greatest sources of happiness, forgiveness and reconciliation is a primary path towards it.

---

14 Luke 15.11-32

14

Enough is enough

Repeatedly throughout this book we have come up against the dilemma of whether happiness is best served by material or moral/spiritual well-being and my bias has been towards the moral and spiritual, although I recognise that we need both. Now, in this penultimate chapter, I want to try to unravel the problem a little more in relation to our personal, corporate and national lives, since happiness is a corporate enterprise as well as a personal one.

At the crudest level we are all familiar with cautionary tales of people who win the lottery only to find that prodigious wealth leads them into a downward spiral of broken relationship, uncontrolled indulgence, and misery. How do they manage it, we ask incredulously. If only I had a bigger house, a higher income, a bigger pension, I could live happily ever after. But does more mean happier? Whatever we have there are advertisers and competitors telling us we need more. Yet happiness is not a material status but a state of mind. Obviously the starving man is less happy than the man who can afford a meal, and the person who has a house is happier than the person who is homeless, but happiness doesn't run parallel with the accrual of wealth, and sometimes can be inverse to it because of the anxieties of investing and managing your money. A bit more space, a bit more disposable income, is absolutely no guarantee of extra happiness. We all know that the photos in *Hello* Magazine, holiday brochures, and car magazines are a mirage of airbrushed perfection, and that behind the posing socialites, the smart venues,

and the shining status symbols is very often a profound dissatisfaction and ennui.

The Camel and the Eye of a Needle

One of Jesus' most catchy phrases is that it is easier for a camel to go through the eye of a needle than for a rich man to enter the kingdom of heaven, suggesting that to be seduced by wealth is to enter a cul-de-sac on the spiritual road. To see their chances of heaven so reduced can seem, to the growing number of wealthy people in Europe and the US, both unfair and an unjust judgement on many generous and good lives. Where would we be without benefactors and charitable donors? It can also seem economically naïve: to make a virtue out of being content with enough, it could be argued, is to take away the motivation and economic driver of the very capitalism that creates the wealth needed to relieve the poor and alleviate the social deprivations that religion prophesies against.

Jesus was not an economist. His point is that, for our spiritual and moral development, we need to be able to recognise and value ourselves stripped of the protective wrapping of possession. Where is the real *me* beneath my public image, my CV, my status represented by house and car, family, and club membership? If you remove all the layers of acquisition you have amassed over a lifetime, you find a different person, not necessarily a more vulnerable one, but the true person, which is what God values and maybe the person that stands the greater chance of happiness. Alain de Botton, in his book *Status Anxiety*[15], captures this in a poignant image when he writes that our worldly status returns to zero when we are in our pyjamas in the terminal ward of a hospital. That picture is the antithesis of the lottery winning, body-beautiful, celebrity culture, extolled in the media. No wonder hospitals and dying are wherever possible hidden and only spoken of in a conspiratorial whisper. They threaten to pull down the golden calf.

Jesus tells a story[16] of a wealthy landowner who was producing more crops than his barns could hold. So, with an eye to long-term security and maybe early retirement in which he could 'eat, drink and be merry', he decided to pull down his barns and build larger ones. 'But God said to him, 'You fool! This very night your life is being demanded of you. And the things you have prepared, whose will they be?' So it is with those who store up treasures for themselves but are not rich toward God'.

The Tall City of Glass that is the Laboratory of the Spirit

I have met many high earning and successful people who say that while material success brings many benefits, it

---

15 *Status Anxiety*, Alain de Botton – Hamish Hamilton Ltd 2004
16 Luke 12

often fails to deliver inner fulfilment, and that, as a way of finding fulfilment, they would like nothing better than to 'give something back to the community'. Often they don't, of course, because the demands of sustaining a wealthy lifestyle – several houses, staff, school fees, boat, holidays, memberships – keep them on the treadmill. Once you've got it, it's hard to give it up and it's not just you, they plead, it's your family and children who depend on you to maintain the status quo. But many do give back to the community typically by giving money, time and expertise to charity, and some purposefully moderate their lifestyle in order to keep perspective for themselves, and for the development of their children's sense of priorities and future happiness. There's nothing worse than an idle rich spoiled brat.

The Welsh poet, RS Thomas, in his poem *Emerging* writes:

> 'Circular as our way
> is, it leads not back to that snake-haunted
> garden, but onward to the tall city
> of glass that is the laboratory of the spirit'

In these lines the snake-haunted garden is of course Adam and Eve's Garden of Eden, and Thomas is suggesting that in the search for understanding and spirituality, which often leads us round in circles, we should not go backwards towards that imagined paradise, but forwards to make sense of all contemporary challenges. The tall city of glass isn't the cathedral of stained glass; it's the skyscraper skyline of reflective buildings that house the banks and the head offices of mega corporations. The word *laboratory* suggests experiment, a place of discovery. Here spiritual and ethical values have to be hammered out in prophetic counterpoint with the iconic celebration of material wealth that the buildings represent.

The tall city of glass is also an icon of globalisation, the phenomenon brought about by satellite communication, multi-nationals and jet travel, in which, on the one hand, you have the same shopping chains in every major city, known as *McDonaldization,* and, on the other, the clash of cultures as, finding themselves in close proximity, ideologies vie for world domination. The terrorist attack of 11 September 2001 is an example of the latter and was, poignantly, an attack on the tall city of glass. So in a globalised world it is hard to see that human happiness can be achieved except by macro decision-making by governments and multi-national corporations, but these rely on electors and shareholders whose superficial interest at elections and annual meetings remains profit.

Happiness requires the human condition to be viewed not only from the global perspective, where individual suffering can be lost because it is too small to get on the screen, but also in the most intimate detail. When people become statistics, no one cares much what happens to them; it is only when we get close enough to identify with their plight, and to hear their cries, that compassion stirs. But even here, as we observed in Thinking about Suffering, it would be patronising to suppose that people cannot be happy and content in adversity.

Make Poverty History

The drive for better life and greater happiness is to some degree a prophetic activity powered not so much by governments as by voluntary organisations and charities. The Make Poverty History initiative is the largest coalition ever assembled in the UK to call for an end to global poverty. Over one hundred charities, organisations and celebrities are working together to bring massive public pressure on the UK government to address the key causes of world poverty: tackling unfair global trade rules, cancelling the debts of the poorest countries and increasing the quality and amount of aid given to developing countries.

Environment

The Christian theology of the environment is based on two principles. First, the Biblical belief that God created a beautiful, well-resourced world for humans to flourish in; with the reciprocal expectation that humans will be good stewards of the Earth, taking responsibility for it as settlers and farmers. And secondly, that happiness grows from contentment rather that greed and avarice. Jesus' teaching often strikes me as blunt and uncompromising. No gentle coaxing of his fragile listeners: 'And do not keep striving for what you are to eat and what you are to drink, and do not keep worrying. For it is the nations of the world that strive after all these things ... Instead, strive for his kingdom, and these things will be given to you as well.'[17] That last sentence is one of the most telling in the New Testament: live by God's values and the rest of the jigsaw will fall into place.

When I visited India with the England Cricket Team in 1992, which I suppose is the equivalent of touring with a Major League baseball team, while watching the BBC World Service TV in my Calcutta hotel room I was surprised by repeated propaganda warnings about the dangers to the environment of air travel. It seemed ironical to be broadcasting this in the third world, but not back in the UK, which has the busiest airport in the world, and where

---

17 Luke 12.29-31

a high percentage of food is imported by air so that we can eat strawberries, cucumbers and exotic fruit all year round. Only now are the facts of airplane pollution becoming common knowledge both in the UK and worldwide, as statistics show that carbon emissions are increasing to dangerously high levels which threaten the whole planet.

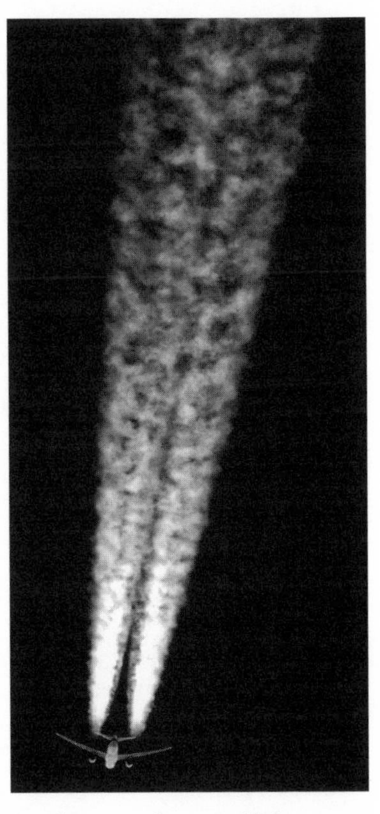

If living within your means and living with respect for the environment has meaning at the level of personal ethics and happiness, then it must also be true at the national and global levels. There is surely a duty of care towards the future. An extraordinary ethical black hole for humanity has emerged at the beginning of the twenty-first century; our generation is consuming the world's resources without really thinking about what will happen to our children and grandchildren. Even if we are conscious of these dangers, we might bury our heads in the sand and argue that alternative, more effective technologies will soon be developed to harness sources of energy other than fossil fuels, or that climate change isn't really so bad after all, or that climate change may be the result of all sorts of naturally occurring events. An even bigger problem is that Western governments believe it would be political suicide to propose a reduction in their peoples' standard of living by rationing fuel. If rich nations were to slash energy consumption, they'd have to go easy on all the luxuries we regard as necessities: refrigerators, cars, air-conditioning, washing machines and television sets; if poor nations did the same, hundreds of millions of people would have to live without even an electric light bulb. Agreements such Kyoto Protocol on Greenhouse gas emissions are a step in the right direction, but Australia and the US did not support it and other countries only agreed to aim at an 8 per cent reduction, which is minuscule in the scale of things.

Figures from the *Jubilee* movement for the cancellation of world debt highlight some startling equations:

money owed by the world's poorest and most indebted nations – $422 billion

money spent by Western industrialised nations on weapons and soldiers each year – $422 billion

money estimated by UN to curb AIDS in Africa – $15 billion

interest needed by African countries to service their foreign debt per annum – $13.5 billion

In the ecology debate in the US Christianity hasn't been entirely on the side of the angels either. Fundamentalist belief in the imminent coming of God and the Last Judgement, of being caught up in the 'Rapture', has meant that Christians of that persuasion have little interest in environmental matters, or even political change, because they think the present order only has to survive about another twenty years or so before the world order ends and God's kingdom comes.

Paradox

As we have seen in the course of this whole discussion of happiness, Christian theology and ethics lives with many paradoxes and feeds off the creative tension that they generate. Indeed, there's a joke that goes: if you've got a theological headache, take Paradox. Of course, it isn't a unique feature of Christianity, but in the light of Jesus' propensity in the Gospel narratives for turning the traditional values of his society upside down, it does seem to me a distinctive characteristic. It's a word that has cropped up repeatedly in these pages: in thinking about suffering as part of the salvation process, in the discussions about the beatitudes and losing your life to save it, and in relation to the constant tension between wealth and poverty, material and spiritual values. I said at the beginning that we only know happiness in contrast to unhappiness or other emotions of sadness, disappointment, and loss and this is true of life generally, always complex and many faceted, full of ambiguities, mysteries and enigmas: doubt and faith; hope and despair; tears and laughter.

And so to my final paradox.

15
Chocolate

I began with Plato and I end with Bridget Jones, Helen Fielding's over-weight, thirty-something, single girl in search of a life, played in the movies by Renée Zellweger. She counters the unhappiness of inadequate relationship with self-indulgent consolation. It could be chocolate, or gin, or shopping, or a reckless fling. Is this so awful? Having described a way of happiness rigorous in rejecting consolation, there needs to be room for imperfection and for taking into account our propensity to mess up. We're only human after all.

What I have been trying to do is to distil the principles of happiness, which could be summed up as: realism about what's possible, appreciation of others and the environment, relationship, virtue, and purpose. My proposals have at times taken little account of human weakness because

there seems no point in compromise when you are trying to set out ideals. Jesus ends the Sermon on the Mount by saying, 'Be ye therefore perfect even as your heavenly father is perfect' and I wonder why we should we aim for anything less.

But between the idea and the reality falls the shadow, the shadow of our moral frailty. Should chocolate therefore be banned, in a get-behind-me-Satan sort of way? That's far too puritan and prissy and I'd hate you to think me a goody two shoes, or whatever the male equivalent is. No, it remains a pleasing confection, a treat, and if the quality's fine enough, actually good for you, they say. What it must not become is my *life*. Chocolate is good (and when I say 'chocolate' I mean a whole expanding metaphor of indulgence), but it's incidental to the main goal of happiness and we must show some degree of realism about it, recognising its gratification limits, if it is to give us genuine pleasure. Binge on it and you'll simply be sick.

There's a rabbinical saying that on the day of judgement, we'll be judged for *pleasures we have refused*, because to refuse opportunities for happiness is to spurn God's bounty and to show a degree of mean-mindedness towards the creator. If this is to mean anything radical then the pleasures we embrace will include the occasional indulgence, spree, and letting down of the hair. Besides, we are happy to celebrate a birthday or an achievement with champagne or theatre tickets we can scarcely afford. And if the path of virtue and self-giving can sometimes seem a too narrow and controlled road to happiness, then we must also learn to let go: relax, enjoy.

So may you be happy, may you find fulfilment, but don't confuse happiness with being on a constant high; try to find a deep underlying contentment that will see you through difficult times as well as good.

Christianity in 10 minutes

Brian Mountford

The best short guide to serious Christianity you will find

You want to know about Christianity? Maybe you've visited a church or cathedral or looked at religious paintings in an art gallery and wondered what the meaning is behind them, why they evoke some sense of mystery and wonder. This short, but profound, "ten minute guide" will help begin to unfold that mystery. Starting with the gospel story, it moves on to the intuitive response to God, the desire for meaning, and how the story can change your life. It answers for the modern reader the lawyer's question to Jesus; "What must I do to inherit eternal life?"

Subjects covered: What is Christianity? Does it work? Can it make you a happier person? Is the Bible true? Do you have to believe in miracles? Do you need to go to Church?

If you want to begin at the beginning with the Christian faith, I can't think of a better way than by sitting down and reading this little book through. Plain-spoken, straightforward, succinct, here is a fresh introduction to the essentials-what Christians believe, how and why they believe what they do, what difference it can all make. If you've been around churches all your life and never fully grasped what it's all about, this is a superb refresher. If Christian faith is brand new to you, what a helpful first step you're holding in your hands. Rev. Dr. Sam Lloyd, Dean of the National Cathedral, Washington DC

The most valuable 10 minutes you will spend this year. Gospel truth. The essence of Christianity, simply and memorably explained. Read it. Peter Bennett-Jones, Chair of Comic Relief

Could not have been published at a more propitious time in world temporal and religious affairs. Canon Mountford sets forth the essentials of Christian truth that transcend reality. In doing so he aids the preachers whose adherence to inerrancy does more to diminish than to fortify and reinforce it. Alexander Kern, Professor of Theology, University of Illinois

Canon Brian Mountford is Vicar of the University Church in Oxford, one of the most visited churches in England.

1 905047 09 6
$8.95/£6.99

Good As New

A radical re-telling of the Christian Scriptures

John Henson

This radical new translation conveys the early Christian scriptures in the idiom of today. It is "inclusive," following the principles which Jesus adopted in relation to his culture. It is women, gay and sinner friendly. It follows principles of cultural and contextual translation. It also returns to the selection of books that modern scholarship now agrees were held in most esteem by the early Church.

A presentation of extraordinary power. Rowan Williams, Archbishop of Canterbury

I can't rate this version of the Christian scriptures highly enough. It is amazingly fresh, imaginative, engaging and bold. Adrian Thatcher, Professor of Applied Theology, College of St Mark and St John, Plymouth

I found this a literally shocking read. It made me think, it made me laugh, it made me cry, it made me angry and it made me joyful. It made me feel like an early Christian hearing these texts for the first time. Elizabeth Stuart, Professor of Christian Theology, King Alfred's College, Winchester

It spoke to me with a powerful relevancy that challenged me to re-think all the things that I have been taught. Tony Campolo, Professor Emeritus of Sociology, Eastern University

With an extraordinary vigour and immediacy, Good As New *constantly challenges, surprises and delights you. Over and over again you feel like you're reading about Jesus for the first time.* Ship of Fools

John Henson, a retired evangelical Baptist minister, has co-ordinated this translation over the last 12 years on behalf of *ONE for Christian Exploration*, a network of radical Christians and over twenty organisations in the UK

1-903816-74-2
£19.99/$29.95 hb

1-90504711-8
£11.99/$19.95 pb

Tomorrow's Christian

Adrian B. Smith

What are the sources of true Christianity? Tradition or Scripture? Experience? How far should our interpretation accommodate modern knowledge?

Some take refuge in fundamentalism, others in emotion, many are leaving the Church. But there are others, called here "tomorrow's Christian", who struggle to bring together in a meaningful way traditional Christianity and a contemporary, nourishing understanding and expression of it.

36 short chapters sum up the characteristics of tomorrow's Christian. One who is questioning, ecologically aware, global, evolving, non-theistic, balanced, right-brain, scriptural, prophetic, peace-making, forgiving, empowered, Jesus-following, seeking, free, discerning, post-modernist, meditating, mystical and others. Ideal for discussion groups, and all individuals looking outside their churches for a way to live as Christians.

An inspiring and multi-faceted vision of "tomorrow's Christian." The layout with many short chapters makes the book easy to read and digest. I enjoyed reading this book immensely. I find it stimulating and encouraging.
Philip Sheppard, *Christians Awakening to a New Awareness*

Adrian B. Smith was ordained as a Roman Catholic priest in 1955.

1 903816 97 1
£9.99/$15.95

The Thoughtful Guide to Faith
Tony Windross

This book is for anyone who would like to take faith seriously but finds their intelligence getting in the way. It outlines, in 37 short chapters, many of the objections raised to formal Christian religion, and suggests ways of dealing with them which do not compromise people's intellectual integrity.

The claim made here is that Christianity is far more about the way we live than the way we think, that faith can work for all of us, and that what we may or may not believe must never be allowed to get in the way of faith.

"A *bombe surprise*, unexpectedly lively, adventurous and radical." Don Cupitt, Emmanuel College, Cambridge

Tony Windross is an Anglican minister in Norfolk, England, with degrees from Cambridge University.

1-903816-68-8
£9.99/$14.95

O

is a symbol of the world, of oneness and unity. O Books explores the many paths of wholeness and spiritual understanding which different traditions have developed down the ages. It aims to bring this knowledge in accessible form, to a general readership, providing practical spirituality to today's seekers.

For the full list of over 200 titles covering:
ACADEMIC/THEOLOGY • ANGELS • ASTROLOGY/NUMEROLOGY • BIOGRAPHY/AUTOBIOGRAPHY • BUDDHISM/ENLIGHTENMENT • BUSINESS/LEADERSHIP/WISDOM • CELTIC/DRUID/PAGAN • CHANNELLING • CHRISTIANITY; EARLY • CHRISTIANITY; TRADITIONAL • CHRISTIANITY; PROGRESSIVE • CHRISTIANITY; DEVOTIONAL • CHILDREN'S SPIRITUALITY • CHILDREN'S BIBLE STORIES • CHILDREN'S BOARD/NOVELTY • CREATIVE SPIRITUALITY • CURRENT AFFAIRS/RELIGIOUS • ECONOMY/POLITICS/SUSTAINABILITY • ENVIRONMENT/EARTH • FICTION • GODDESS/FEMININE • HEALTH/FITNESS • HEALING/REIKI • HINDUISM/ADVAITA/VEDANTA • HISTORY/ARCHAEOLOGY • HOLISTIC SPIRITUALITY • INTERFAITH/ECUMENICAL • ISLAM/SUFISM • JUDAISM/CHRISTIANITY • MEDITATION/PRAYER • MYSTERY/PARANORMAL • MYSTICISM • MYTHS • POETRY • RELATIONSHIPS/LOVE • RELIGION/PHILOSOPHY • SCHOOL TITLES • SCIENCE/RELIGION • SELF-HELP/PSYCHOLOGY • SPIRITUAL SEARCH • WORLD RELIGIONS/SCRIPTURES • YOGA

Please visit our website, www.O-books.net